E&L1/RetDat

Bonnie
Prince
Charlie

Barbara Mure Rasmusen

First published in Great Britain by Heinemann Library
Halley Court, Jordan Hill, Oxford OX2 8EJ
a division of Reed Educational and Professional Publishing Ltd

OXFORD FLORENCE PRAGUE MADRID ATHENS
MELBOURNE AUCKLAND KUALA LUMPUR SINGAPORE TOKYO
IBADAN NAIROBI KAMPALA JOHANNESBURG GABORONE
PORTSMOUTH NH (USA) CHICAGO MEXICO CITY SAO PAULO

Printed in China

00 99 98 97 96
10 9 8 7 6 5 4 3 2 1

ISBN 0 431 05885 7
This title is also available in a hardback library edition (ISBN 0 431 07873 4).

British Library Cataloguing in Publication Data
Rasmusen, Barbara
Bonnie Prince Charlie. – (Scottish history topics)
1. Charles Edward Stuart, Prince, 1720–1788 – Juvenile literature 2. Pretenders to the throne –
Scotland – Biography – Juvenile literature
3. Scotland – History – 18th century – Juvenile literature
I. Title
941.1'072'092

Acknowledgements
The Publishers would like to thank the following for permission to reproduce photographs:
British Museum: p.9 top, p.17 bottom; City of Edinburgh Museums & Galleries: p.8 top;
Thomas Coram Foundation for Children: p.11; Dundee Art Galleries: p.20; Mary Evans
Picture Library: p.7 bottom, p.19 bottom; Hulton Picture Company: p.18; National Galleries
of Scotland: p.1, p.10, p.16, p.17 centre; Royal Collection, St James's Palace © HM The Queen:
p.9 bottom, p.14; Scotland in Focus: p.5 both, p.6 left and right, p.7 top, p.12 all, p.13 all,
p.15 left and bottom, p.19 top.

Cover photograph reproduced with permission of The Royal Collection, © Her Majesty
Queen Elizabeth II.

Our thanks to Meg Lorimer of Burgh Primary School, Galashiels for her comments in the
preparation of this book.

Every effort has been made to contact copyright holders of any material reproduced in this
book. Any omissions will be rectified in subsequent printings if notice is given to the
Publisher.

Contents

The beginning of the rebellion

The Jacobite cause

In 1745, Prince Charles Edward Stuart began his short but now famous trip to Scotland to reclaim the throne of Great Britain. The throne had been lost to the Stuarts by his grandfather, James II. James II had been forced to leave England in 1688 because of the way he had ruled. Charles' father, James III, had tried to reclaim the throne from Queen Anne in 1708 and from George I in 1715. He and his **Jacobite supporters** were not successful. In 1745 Charles, with the help of the King of France, Louis XIV, was determined to try again. Louis was willing to help Charles because he wanted a Catholic king to rule in Britain.

Louis sent **spies** to England. They returned and said that there were many Englishmen who would welcome Charles and fight for the Jacobite cause. Some Scottish **chiefs** had also said that they would help Charles and join in a Jacobite **rebellion**.

The coming of the prince

Louis gathered together an army of 10,000 troops at Dunkirk in 1744 but all their ships were wrecked in a storm. The French

invasion never took place but Charles was still very determined to claim the British throne. In 1745 he and a company of French **volunteers** set sail for Scotland in two ships, the *Elizabeth* and the *Doutelle*. A British warship attacked them. Neither side won, but the ships were badly damaged. The larger ship, the *Elizabeth*, returned to France with the volunteers and most of the weapons. Charles, with seven supporters, sailed on to Scotland. He landed first at Eriskay and then, on 25 July 1745, at Loch nan Uamh, near Arisaig.

ABOVE AND LEFT: The Scottish chiefs wrote to Charles telling him not to come without an army of 6000 French soldiers. He did not receive the letter. He landed on the rocky shores of Loch nan Uamh with only seven supporters – the Seven Men of Moidart.

The gathering of the clans

RIGHT:
The Jacobite **Monument** at Glenfinnan. The clans gathered here to support Charles Edward Stuart and the Jacobite rebellion.

BELOW:
Linlithgow. Prince Charles and his army camped here for one night on the way to Edinburgh.

The **clan chiefs**, Macleod and Macdonald of Sleat, knew that Charles was coming to Scotland. When he arrived without the 6000 French soldiers, they said that they would not fight for him. Charles then persuaded two local chiefs, Cameron of Locheil and Macdonald of Clanranald, to support him. Charles sent a message to all the other clan chiefs asking them to come to Glenfinnan on 19 August 1745 to start the **rebellion**.

Glenfinnan
Charles himself arrived at 11 o'clock in the morning with 150 men. The Laird of Morar was waiting with another 150 men. It seemed that no other **clansmen** were coming. Then, in the distance, the sound of **bagpipes** was heard. Over the nearby hill came 700 Cameron clansmen. More clansmen arrived. The red and white **Jacobite standard** was raised. The clansmen shouted, 'Prince Charles, King of the **Gael**.' The rebellion had begun with about 1200 men.

The Pass of Corriearrick

When Sir John Cope, the **commander** of the **government** army in Scotland, heard about the clans gathering he set off for **Fort** Augustus. This was an army fort in the west. He wanted to stop the rebellion. Part of his route was a twisting road through the **Pass** of Corriearrick.

Charles decided that the pass would be a good place to attack Cope and his men. Cope heard of Charles' plan. He knew that he and his men would be in great danger so he marched north-eastward to Inverness instead. This meant that there were no troops to stop Charles and his men marching to Perth. From there they went to Stirling, Linlithgow and Corstorphine to attack Edinburgh.

ABOVE:
These actors are dressed in Highland clothes and are using weapons which would have been used by the Jacobites.

LEFT:
Charles ordered the red and white Jacobite standard to be raised on 19 August 1745. Charles was dressed in a brown coat, scarlet breeches and a yellow waistcoat.

Won – a city and a battle

ABOVE:
While Prince Charles was at Edinburgh he was charming to everyone. This picture, painted in the 19th century, shows him surrounded by people who admired and respected him.

RIGHT:
Sir John Cope thought that the Jacobite army would be easily beaten. This cartoon shows him running away, defeated by the Jacobites' first fierce charge.

The Camerons waited in hiding beside one of the city gates. A group of townspeople came out of this gate to discuss the surrender of the city. When their **coach** returned, the gate was opened to let it in. The Camerons **charged** with it into the city. They had taken the city of Edinburgh by early morning.

The government troops locked themselves inside Edinburgh Castle. They would not let the **Jacobites** in. Charles rode into Edinburgh on 17 September to be met by cheering crowds. They saw a tall young man who was very good looking and named him 'Bonnie Prince Charlie'.

There were two **regiments** of **government** troops guarding Edinburgh in September 1745. Charles asked the people of Edinburgh to **surrender**. They refused, so he sent 900 Cameron **clansmen** to take the city.

A Race from Preston Pans to Berwick.

'The first general that ever was a messenger of his own defeat.'

LEFT:
Charles rode through the streets of Edinburgh among cheering crowds. He was delighted to be in command of the Scottish capital.

BELOW:
Before he fought in the battle of Prestonpans, Prince Charlie held a grand ball in this room – the Great Gallery at Holyroodhouse.

The Battle – Prestonpans

Sir John Cope, the government **commander**, had sailed from Aberdeen to try to reach Edinburgh before the Jacobites. He arrived at Dunbar on 18 September 1745 and began to march towards Edinburgh. Cope's army met the Jacobite army at Prestonpans on 21 September. The Jacobite army attacked early in the morning. Their first charge forced the government troops back to a long wall which was too high to climb. Hundreds of them were trapped there and were killed. The battle was won by the Jacobites in less than ten minutes.

The march into England

After the **Jacobite victory** at Prestonpans, Prince Charles wanted to march to London at once. He wanted to rule all of Great Britain, not just Scotland. However, the Highland **clansmen** did not want to march southwards. Some of them went home for the winter, but they were replaced by more **clans** who joined in the **rebellion**. At the end of October there were 5000 soldiers and 500 horsemen in the Jacobite army. Prince Charles now persuaded his **supporters** to attack England on 8 November 1745.

Unexpected success

Two **government** armies were sent to fight against Prince Charles. One army marched to Newcastle and the other guarded the London road. The first was led by George Wade. The second was led by the Duke of Cumberland, the king's son. Lord George Murray was Prince Charles's most experienced **commander**. He suggested that the Jacobite army should avoid a battle with Wade at Newcastle by marching through the west of the country. Charlie agreed and his army marched to Carlisle. After a short **siege** the commander of Carlisle, Colonel Durant, **surrendered** the town and the castle to Prince Charles.

God grant that Marshal Wade
May by thy mighty aid
  Victory bring.
May he sedition hush
And like a torrent rush
Rebellious Scots to crush.
  God save the King.

From France and Pretender
Great Britain defend her,
  Foes let them fall;
From foreign slavery,
Priests and their knavery,
And Popish reverie,
  God save us all.

The Jacobites marched southwards. On 28 November they captured Manchester. They then pretended to be heading for Wales. The Duke of Cumberland moved his army to attack them, but he had been tricked. At the last moment the Jacobites turned towards Derby. They reached it on 4 December.

The retreat

At Derby, Lord George Murray gave Prince Charles a warning. The Jacobite army of less than 6000 men would have to fight against 30,000 government troops before they could reach London. They had to **retreat** as quickly as they could.

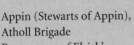

Jacobite Regiments that took part in the 1745 Rebellion

Appin (Stewarts of Appin),	Lady Mackintosh's
Atholl Brigade	MacLachlan's
Bannerman of Elsick's	Maclean's
Cameron of Lochiel's	MacLeod of Raasay's
Chisholm of Strathglass'	Macpherson of Cluny's
Duke of Perth's	Manchester
Earl of Cromartie's	Monaltrie's and Balmoral
Forfarshire (Ogilvy's)	Roy Stewart's (Edinburgh)
Frasers of Lovat	Stoneywood's (Aberdeen)
Gordon of Glenbucket's	
Lord Lewis Gordon's	**Cavalry:**
Grants of Glenmoriston	FitzJames' Horse
Grante's Artillery	Hussars
Irish Piquets	Kilmarnock's Horse
MacDonald of Clanranald's	The Lifeguards (Elcho's Troop,
MacDonald of Glencoe's	Balmerino's Troop)
MacDonell of Glengarry's	Perthshire Horse
MacDonell of Keppoch's	(Strathallan's)
MacGregor's ·	Pitsligo's Horse
Mackinnon's	Royal Scots (French)

LEFT:
This picture shows English soldiers leaving the **turnpike** at Tottenham Court Road to march to a camp at Finchley. There they got ready to fight against the Jacobites.

Retreat!

RIGHT:
Prince Charles
wanted to
capture Stirling
Castle before
Henry Hawley
and his
government
troops reached it.
He did not
manage to do so.

The **Jacobite retreat** from Derby began on 6 December 1745. Lord George Murray and the other Jacobite leaders had persuaded Prince Charles to return to Scotland. They did not know that Londoners thought Prince Charles and his Jacobite army would arrive soon and take the city, and that in London King George II had a ship ready to escape to Germany.

ABOVE:
Drumlanrig
Castle. Prince
Charles and his
army stopped at
this castle as they
made their way
to Glasgow.

RIGHT:
Inverness Castle
was knocked
down by the
Jacobites in
February 1746.

The Jacobites only knew that there were too many **government** troops ready to fight them. The march back to Scotland was difficult. Prince Charles felt he had been **betrayed** by Lord George Murray. He became moody and tried to slow down the retreat, walking behind the army or sometimes riding on a black horse through the **clansmen**, scattering them.

Small groups of the Duke of Cumberland's 6000 troops caught up with them. Lord George Murray fought off an attack at the rear of the marchers, at Clifton near Penrith, on 18 December 1745.

On 20 December 1745, the Jacobites crossed the River Esk, back into Scotland. The Jacobite army now had 4000 troops. They marched to Glasgow and then to Stirling. More Scotsmen joined them until there were nearly 8000 men in their army. This army defeated government troops, led by Henry Hawley, at Falkirk on 17 January 1746. So the British government sent the Duke of Cumberland to Scotland to deal with the rebels. The Jacobite army retreated to the Highlands, although that was not what Prince Charles wanted. They reached Inverness on 17 February 1746 and captured it the following day.

BELOW:
Blair Castle was attacked by the Jacobite army.

BELOW LEFT:
Kilravock Castle. Here Prince Charles ate a simple meal before the Battle of Culloden.

LEFT:
The battlefield of Culloden. The ground was flat and open. The Highlanders liked to fight on hilly ground where they could **ambush** *their enemy from a higher level.*

Culloden – 1746

RIGHT:
The Duke of Cumberland allowed the **slaughter** *of the dying and the captured. He earned the nickname 'The Butcher'.*

BELOW:
The government troops fired or stabbed at the bodies of the clansmen.

Prince Charles and his army remained at Inverness from 17 February to 14 April. The Duke of Cumberland and his **government** troops moved slowly northwards. They reached Nairn on 14 April 1746. Prince Charles and his generals expected Cumberland to attack them on 15 April. Against the advice of Lord George Murray and the **chiefs**, Charles chose open moorland near Culloden House as the best place for the battle.

15 April 1746

On 15 April the **Jacobite** army stood ready to fight at Culloden, but Cumberland's army did not come. That night the Jacobites tried to make a surprise attack by marching to Nairn. They did not reach Nairn by morning and had to return to Culloden. Although the Jacobites were exhausted and hungry, the two armies met the next day.

BELOW:
The monument at Culloden, and what is written on it.

THE BATTLE OF CULLODEN WAS FOUGHT ON THIS MOOR 16TH APRIL 1746.

THE GRAVES OF THE GALLANT HIGHLANDERS WHO FOUGHT FOR SCOTLAND & PRINCE CHARLIE ARE MARKED BY THE NAMES OF THEIR CLANS.

16 April 1746

The flatness of the moor made it possible for the government cannons to be fired at the **clansmen** from a distance. Many were killed. When the survivors made a **charge** towards the government army they were shot and killed in large numbers as they ran forward. The battle lasted less than an hour – 1000 clansmen lay dead.

ABOVE:
*This picture, from January 1747, shows a clansman shooting an army captain with the captain's own pistol. It tried to show that all clansmen were **treacherous** and deserved to be killed.*

LEFT:
Thirty Jacobite officers and men hid in the barn of Old Leanach Cottage. They were burnt to death by Cumberland's men after the Battle of Culloden.

After the battle

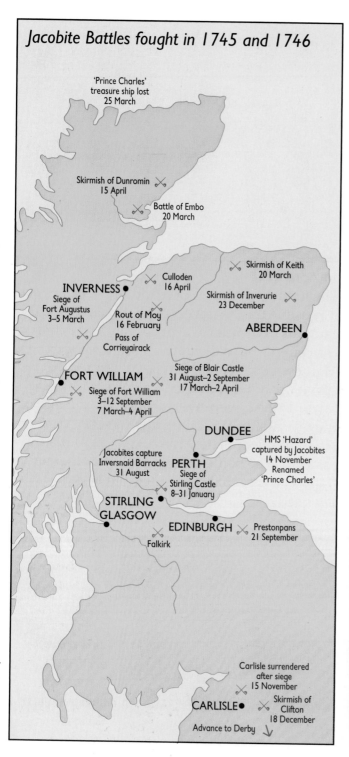

Jacobite Battles fought in 1745 and 1746

'Prince Charles' treasure ship lost 25 March

Skirmish of Dunromin 15 April

Battle of Embo 20 March

Skirmish of Keith 20 March

Culloden 16 April

Skirmish of Inverurie 23 December

INVERNESS
Siege of Fort Augustus 3–5 March

Rout of Moy 16 February

Pass of Corrieyairack

ABERDEEN

FORT WILLIAM
Siege of Fort William 3–12 September 7 March–4 April

Siege of Blair Castle 31 August–2 September 17 March–2 April

DUNDEE

HMS 'Hazard' captured by Jacobites 14 November Renamed 'Prince Charles'

Jacobites capture Inversnaid Barracks 31 August

PERTH
Siege of Stirling Castle 8–31 January

STIRLING
GLASGOW

EDINBURGH
Prestonpans 21 September

Falkirk

Carlisle surrendered after siege 15 November

CARLISLE
Skirmish of Clifton 18 December

Advance to Derby

The Duke of Cumberland and his men showed no mercy to the defeated **clansmen**. The men who lay dying on the battlefield of Culloden were stabbed to death or left to die in agony. In the countryside around Culloden, **innocent** men, women and children were attacked and killed.

The fate of the Jacobites

During the three months after the battle, Cumberland's men took 3470 prisoners. Some of them were **executed**. Some were sent abroad to be sold as slaves. Some returned to their homes to find them burned and their possessions stolen. The surviving clansmen were not allowed to wear **tartan** or play the **bagpipes**. After 1747 the **clan chiefs** lost the right to be chiefs. A way of life and a people were nearly destroyed.

The flight of Bonnie Prince Charlie

Prince Charles left the battlefield at Culloden and travelled 15 miles south-west to Gortaleg House. This was the home of Lord Lovat.

Lord Lovat wanted him to fight again but Prince Charles received a letter from Lord George Murray which blamed him, Charles, for the failure of the **rebellion**. He decided not to continue.

Prince Charles set sail on 25 April to the Western Isles. The sea was stormy and he had to land on Benbecula. He and his companions spent the next few months travelling from island to island. They lived on food which they hunted or which was given to them. They seldom slept in a house. **Government** ships and troops were sent to capture Prince Charles. The islanders helped him and he managed to stay free. On 20 June he met Flora Macdonald, the woman who was to help him reach a safer place – the Isle of Skye.

LEFT:
Flora Macdonald lived in this cottage on Skye.

LEFT INSET:
Flora Macdonald was the daughter of Ranald Macdonald of Milton. She was arrested on 8 November 1746 for helping Prince Charles and she was taken to the Tower of London on 6 December. After she was released, she returned to Skye in 1748. She married and had ten children. Flora died in March 1790.

THE AGREABLE CONTRAST.

LEFT:
This picture was drawn to show what the Jacobites thought of the Duke of Cumberland.

LEFT CENTRE:
Flora meets Prince Charles.

Escape to the Isle of Skye

THE SKYE BOAT SONG
Traditional

CHORUS *Speed bon-nie boat, like a bird on the wing, On-ward the sail-ors cry!*

Car-ry the lad that is born to be king, O-ver the sea to Skye! Skye!

VERSE *Loud the winds howl, Loud the waves roar, thun-der-claps rend the air,*

Baf-fled our foes stand on the shore, Fol-low they will not dare.

2.
Though the waves leap, soft shall ye sleep,
Ocean's a royal bed;
Rocked in the deep, Flora will keep
Watch by your weary head.

CHORUS

3.
Many's the lad fought on that day,
Well the claymore could wield
When the night came, silently lay
Dead on Culloden's field.

CHORUS

4.
Burned are our homes, exile and death
Scatter the loyal men;
Yet, e're the sword cool in the sheath,
Charlie will come again.

CHORUS

RIGHT:
Prince Charles dressed up as Betty Bourke. She was an Irish servant girl, and Flora Macdonald's maid.

Prince Charles had been hunted from island to island by **government** troops. Hugh Macdonald of Armadale, a captain in the government army, secretly wanted to help Prince Charles to escape. It was he who arranged for his step-daughter, Flora Macdonald, to help.

Bonnie Charlie's now awa',
Safely owre the friendly main;
Many a heart will break in twa,
Should he ne're come back again.

Will ye no come back again?
Will ye no come back again?
Better lo'ed ye canna be,
Will ye no come back again?

Flora and her friend, Lady Clanranald, suggested that Prince Charles should dress up as Flora's maid, Betty Bourke. Then he would travel with Flora and her servant, Neil, to Skye. No one could move around the islands without a **travel pass** given to them by government troops. A plan was devised. Flora's step-father, Hugh Macdonald, would stop her on her way to Lady Clanranald's house. He would arrest her and question her as he did all travellers. He would set her free again, pretending that nothing was wrong. He would give her a travel pass for herself, Betty Bourke and Neil. On 28 June 1746 Flora brought the travel passes and women's clothes to Prince Charles at Rossinish. The escape began.

ABOVE:
Sunset over the Isle of Skye.

LEFT:
Prince Charles says goodbye to Flora Macdonald in 1746. This was painted by G.W. Joy.

To return no more

BELOW:
*Prince Charles
leaving Scotland
on 20 September
1746.*

*'When Charlie to
the Highlands
came,
It was all joy and
gladness.
We did not think
our hearts so
soon
Would broken be
with sadness.'
Robert Allan
(1774–1841)*

Flora, Neil and Prince Charles, in his disguise as Betty Bourke, made their way safely to Skye in a rowing boat with a crew of five men. They landed at Kilbride. It was not safe there so they set off for the Isle of Raasay. The people they met on the road were surprised at the way the so-called maid was walking. They reported that they had seen a very big woman who looked like a man in women's clothing and that perhaps it was Bonnie Prince Charlie. It was too dangerous to stay long in Skye. Prince Charles returned to mainland Scotland, landing at Mallaig on 5 July.

Prince Charles spent the next three months in hiding. He lived in caves and on mountainsides. His **Jacobite supporters** looked after him wherever he went. At last he reached Cluny's Cage, a hideout on the slope of Ben Alder. While he was there he heard that some French ships had arrived at Loch nan Uamh. Prince Charles and his companions reached the ships on 19 September 1746. They sailed for France the next day. Charles never returned. He died on 31 January 1788 in Rome, a sad and disappointed old man.

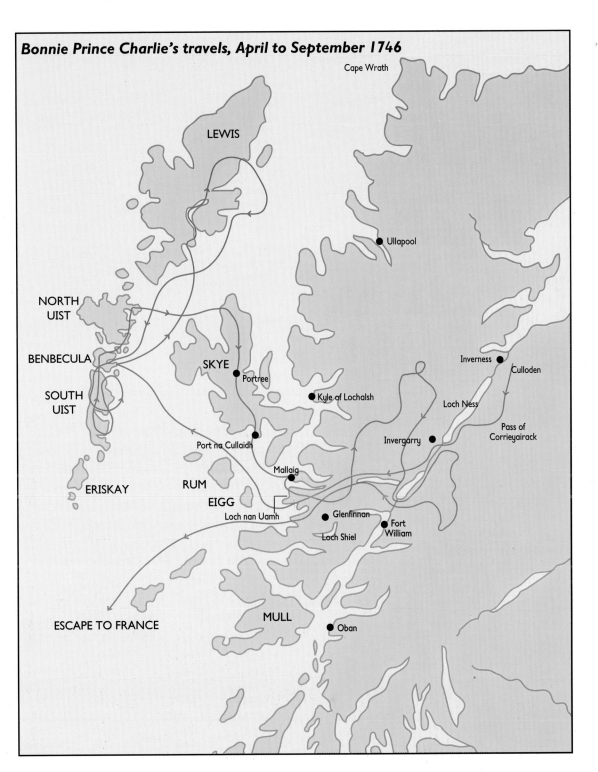

Bonnie Prince Charlie's travels, April to September 1746

Cape Wrath

LEWIS

Ullapool

NORTH
UIST

BENBECULA

SOUTH
UIST

SKYE

Portree

Inverness

Culloden

Kyle of Lochalsh

Loch Ness

Pass of
Corrieyairack

Invergarry

ERISKAY

Port na Cullaidh

RUM

EIGG

Mallaig

Loch nan Uamh

Glenfinnan

Loch Shiel

Fort
William

ESCAPE TO FRANCE

MULL

Oban

Glossary

ambush – attack from a hiding place

bagpipes – a musical instrument made of a bag and pipes. One pipe is used for blowing air into the bag, and the other pipes are used for playing the tune. They were used by clansmen marching into battle.

betray – to be disloyal to

charge – an attack made by running towards the enemy

chief – the leader of a clan

clan – a group of families with the same surname, led by a chief

clansmen – the men in a Scottish clan

coach – a carriage pulled by horses

cockade – a rosette of ribbons or feathers, worn on the hat as a badge

commander – the leader of a group of soldiers

executed – put to death

fort – a building with high walls and few windows, easily defended by the soldiers who live in it

Gael – a Scottish Highlander

Gaelic – the language spoken by some Scottish Highlanders

government – the people ruling over a country

Highlanders – people who live in the north and north-west of Scotland

innocent – having done nothing wrong

invasion – an attack on one country by another country

Jacobite – a follower of James II and his son Charles (Jacobus is another form of James)

monument – a stone pillar or building built to make sure that an event is remembered

pass – a gap in a range of mountains

rebellion – an uprising against the government

regiment – a large group of soldiers

retreat – moving an army back when it is being beaten

siege – the surrounding of a castle, not letting anyone enter or leave

slaughter – to kill in great numbers

spies – people who watch others in secret and try to get information

standard – a flag with an emblem or object on it

supporters – followers of a person or group

surrender – to give up

tartan – a checked cloth worn in Scotland

travel pass – a permit allowing its holder entry into a restricted area

treacherous – not to be trusted

turnpike – a gate where money is paid before people are allowed to travel along a road

victory – a win

volunteer – a person who does something without being asked

Timeline 1745–1746

The Jacobite rebellion

July 1745

16th Prince Charles sets sail for Britain from France.
25th He lands at Loch nan Uamh with only a few troops and weapons.

August 1745

19th The Jacobite Standard is raised at Glenfinnan.

September 1745

17th Bonnie Prince Charlie enters Edinburgh in triumph.
21st A Jacobite victory at Prestonpans.

December 1745

6th The retreat from Derby begins.
20th The Jacobites cross back into Scotland.

November 1745

8th The Jacobites cross the River Esk into England.

October 1745

January 1746

17th The Battle of Falkirk – a Jacobite victory.

February 1746

17th Charles and the Jacobite army capture Inverness.

March 1746

June 1746

20th Prince Charles meets Flora Macdonald, who helps him to escape.

May 1746

April 1746

15th Unsuccessful night march to Nairn.
16th The Battle of Culloden – a Jacobite defeat.
25th Bonnie Prince Charlie sails to the Western Isles of Scotland.

July 1746

August 1746

September 1746

20th Prince Charles leaves Scotland for ever.

Index